paradox hill

FROM APPALACHIA TO LUNAR SHORE

poems by

LOUISE MᶜNEILL

EDITED AND WITH AN INTRODUCTION BY

A. E. STRINGER

Vandalia Press

MORGANTOWN 2009

Vandalia Press, Morgantown, 26506
© 2009 West Virginia University Press

First edition published 1972 by West Virginia University Library
Revised edition 2009
Printed in the United States of America

15 14 13 12 11 10 09   1 2 3 4 5 6 7 8

ISBN-13: 978-1-933202-37-2 (alk. paper)

Cataloguing information for this title can be found at http://loc.gov

Library of Congress Control Number: 2009922292

Contents

Scattered Leaves

Foreword to the First Edition

Long ago, in a book called *Gauley Mountain*, I wrote the lore and language of my people, the Appalachian mountaineers. In this book I have written again of "Gauley," but not of "Gauley" alone. For there has been for me and for all my people that farther journey through the atomic age. We West Virginia mountaineers are Americans, and—like all Americans—we travel far. In these thirty-some years of life, we have gone from the cornfields to the Hiroshima cloud; from blackberry patch to lunar shore.

Here in Appalachia, where many of our yeoman farmers and swift-footed ridge runners have lived on the same patch of ground for eight or nine generations, the memories are long. They move back to the time of the buffalo and wild pigeon, know the Indian war party, and the blue and gray hosts. But we remember, too, the Solomons, Iwo Jima, the Korean reservoir, Vietnam, and the blast-off at the Cape.

In a sense—where the subconscious mind runs deep—all of our experiences are blended and whirled: the Indian signal smoke, the atomic mushroom; the spinning wheel and the cyclotron; the winding wood path and the orbit flame. So Appalachia is not a consistent land—not at all like the hambone and moonshine stereotype. For Appalachia is life, and life is not—cannot be, surely should not be—consistent. Yet the life thread is strong. And here in our mountains it runs from the green savannahs to atom fire.

Introduction

Louise McNeill's poems are like fine antiques: elegant, durable, widely appealing, and never outmoded. In fact, like a vase or quilt that we treasure down the generations, they have an aura of necessity, a lasting presence among the newer, shinier pieces we may read in anthologies today. She reminds us that our place and time on earth are fleeting, and that speaking artfully of the big subjects—God, love, evil, and home—is what we must do.

First published in 1972 by the West Virginia University Library, the major collection of McNeill's mature career, *Paradox Hill,* has too long been out of print. As Appalachian Studies programs rise to prominence at more universities, many valued works of the region are finding new audiences. One needs only to peruse the recent programs of the annual Appalachian Studies Association Conference to realize that such memorable voices as Harriet Arnow, whose collected short stories were released by the University of Michigan Press in 2005, are garnering renewed critical appreciation. That the resurgence of West Virginia University Press as a source for regional literature has coincided with this growth makes perfect sense. And so the time has come for a new edition of Louise McNeill's wonderful book.

These poems are so sturdily constructed that they have survived the changing literary fashions that might seem to render them obsolete. The academic, the beat, the urban, the experimental, the confessional, the international, the post-modern, the performative: these and other trends have shaped the making and valuing of poetry in the new century, but McNeill's work remains powerful because of the craft and devotion she brings to the materials:

> *For now the rain has come at last—*
> *The cool and silver calm,*
> *Whose simple meaning of the past*
> *Is now our only balm.*
> ("Letter Written at Twilight")

With ballad rhythms and modified accentual verse, an insistence on rhyme and repetition, and the liberal use of common speech, her early work, especially, sings to the reader of place and history. She celebrates the Appalachian tradition built on the sweat of families drawing a livelihood from the land. And in *Paradox Hill*, she answers the call to go beyond her region, exploring our human place in a widening universe.

A country soul, Louise McNeill pursued higher learning as a way of enriching herself and her community. Born in Pocahontas County and raised on a hilltop farm, she taught in rural schools in southern West Virginia before her classic *Gauley Mountain* debuted in 1939 to national acclaim. Her verse-history, praised by Stephen Vincent Benet, was celebrated as authentic both in subject and voice, capturing the tensions of memorable characters in a rugged landscape. As poet and McNeill scholar Maggie Anderson has observed in her introduction to *Hill Daughter: New and Selected Poems*, the Appalachian voice has been stereotyped as ignorant, but in McNeill's work, the beauty of speech rhythms and the raw regional dialect are fused into a statelier, subtler poetic idiom: "her best poems are written in a blended language that is colloquial, emotionally complex, and intellectually exacting." In *Paradox Hill*, we find a generous selection of poems in this vein. Consider "The Ballad of Pete Ellers," in which a cruel man hounds a widow to death for the water on her land. McNeill's speaker vividly renders his cruelty in a four-beat, strong-stress rhythm that features just such a blend of language:

Just plain, born meanness it was in Pete,
As if the Devil—He like to beat
His bulls and horses, would take a chain
And stand there lashing, and lash again,
To cut the blood out; then laugh to hear
The wild-horse whicker, to smell the fear.
It gave him pleasure, so it would seem,
To watch things suffer and hear them scream.

The widow Kramer triumphs when her spirit, plucky as ever, returns to haunt Ellers in his old age.

In this and other poems we listen to a voice that poet Irene McKinney, in her essay "The Poet as Teacher," has called "harsh, direct, and force-ful," one that younger poets need to hear because strong work depends on a writer's understanding of the relationship between beauty and toughness. Perhaps it is exactly this voice, direct but not simple, that par-tially explains the fact that McNeill is one of a handful of poets whose work may be found on the adult poetry shelves as well as in the young readers' sections of libraries. In comparing McNeill's "Memoria" to Yeats, McKinney notes how the tough-but-beautiful voice serves the poet's lyric impulse while rejecting the easy comforts of sentimentality:

I have never heard them;
I shall never hear—

Still an echo falling
When the night is clear,
In the darkness wakes me
Like a trumpet's call:
Wild swans crying
Southward in the fall.

As an experienced teacher and poet of rising stature, McNeill saw her poems appear in *Harper's, Atlantic Monthly, Poetry, American Mercury,* and *Commonweal* beside such luminaries as Auden, Yeats, de la Mare, and Jesse Stuart. Her path led to more books, to Master's and Doctoral degrees, to study with Robert Frost, and to professorships at West Virginia University and several other state colleges. In the decades after World War II, she continued to write and publish, and many of the poems in *Paradox Hill* originated in this period. In 1972, a chapbook, *From a Dark Mountain,* appeared from Morris Harvey College in Charleston, West Virginia, containing several poems from the upcoming *Paradox Hill.* While introducing the book, William Plumley noted that these poems brought "a new dimension to her imagination" and that McNeill had by then "lived through the old moralities and the new."

At work late in life on the manuscript for *Fermi Buffalo* (University of Pittsburgh Press, 1994), with the help of writer Topper Sherwood, McNeill availed herself of the common practice of poets of long career, assembling the collection in part from previously published volumes. A few years earlier, Maggie Anderson had helped McNeill compile *Hill Daughter: New and Selected Poems* (University of Pittsburgh Press, 1991). Included in both of these volumes were poems from McNeill's great *Gauley Mountain* (1939), as well as from *Time is Our House* (1942) and *Elderberry Flood* (1976). But both late-career collections selected most liberally from *Paradox Hill,* acknowledging its centrality.

Paradox Hill is in many senses McNeill's richest book, representing a defining turn in her writing. The subtitle itself, "From Appalachia to Lunar Shore," promises a movement beyond her signature subjects. "Appalachia," the book's first section, features work that focuses on McNeill's West Virginia roots, the familiar homespun characters and settings of *Gauley Mountain* and *Time is Our House*. In subsequent sections we see her eye turning, for the first time, to the world beyond, yet without leaving her home behind. In "Scattered Leaves" and "To Lunar Shore," *Paradox Hill*, like her home state, reacts to the powerful influence of science and technology, which—via the airwaves and the new roads—had begun to change the character of the hill country, to deepen and broaden the thinking of its people.

For McNeill, this change was fascinating despite the challenges it presented to traditional mountain culture. Taking the risk of alienating some of her audience, she saw the advent of television, the nuclear age, and space flight as opportunities. As a poet alive to history, a subject she had taught for many years, and perhaps recalling a few critics who had labeled some of her early work as overly pastoral or nostalgic, McNeill resolved to keep mind and senses open to the new shapes of the century. For instance, in "Reflection Without Color," she addresses the diversity of races and cultures against a mid-century background of rising conflict:

We are nothing; we are all—all whose pigments blend and fade.
Where we walk no fern is bended;
Through night's claws we slip unwounded,
Shadows passing into shade:
In God's image we are made—

Having neither shape nor color,
Immaterial as light,
And our only proof of living:
Breath upon the mirror moving—
On the mirror of the night.

Always a woman of faith, she here acknowledges the essence of humanity as begotten of a single Power, one we can't fully know and one that modern physics might illuminate.

"Scattered Leaves" contains a rich variety of poems. Neither strictly narrative nor of scientific bent, they were probably intended by McNeill as transitional. The leaves, evoking a book's pages, remind us that nature's cycle governs all things. The image of darkness recurs throughout this section, sometimes suggesting our ignorance and fear, as in "The Cave," and sometimes suggesting evil, as in "The Golden Garden of Cuzco," when, under "the Sungod's dying rays," virgins of the temple are raped by conquering Europeans. Perhaps because she understood the hardships of nature so well, many of these poems run distinctly counter to the pastoral. Her "Eden Tree" is a symbol filled with woe, yet she praises it for the necessary knowledge of evil it has provided: "as surely praise / Your roothold in the night." Like Adam and Eve, our civilization has no trouble creating its own problems, as her poem "Confession" illustrates. In our ignorance and fear, we may wish to hide from nature and death, to "build the wall / To shield us from the sparrow's fall," and consequently, "faint of hope, [we] dare not forsake / The four-lane boulevard to take / The wild road . . ." Beside the great forces of nature and time, our smallness almost paralyzes us, yet the "wild road" calls. In "Aubade to Fear," where the sparrow's fall reappears, the speaker transcends the anxiety of mortality because she "slept with seeing eyes," recognizing the limits of our new inventions: "how thin the string by which we tie / Our great ships of the wind and sky— / And what a little thing to die."

In exploring the great mysteries, McNeill also peers through the lens of modern science, considered by some of her generation as insufficiently poetic. For her, quantum physics, relativity, and the expanding universe did not represent a threat to belief in a Creator, but instead a new way of seeing the glory of the Creation. In "After Hearing a Lecture on Modern Physics," she observes that the star of Bethlehem sang "the atom's song." Thus, the rustic ballads of "Appalachia" give way in the book's final section to a rhapsodic ranging of language that seeks to render poetically the miracle and message of Creation, from nuclei to galaxies. It is not surprising to note that in 1958 the first major radio telescope of the National Radio Astronomy Observatory was built in McNeill's native Pocahontas County.

The poems in "To Lunar Shore" blend, not always comfortably for her readers, her interest in science—the flashy and dangerous inventions of the twentieth century—and the values most Americans, especially Appalachians, held sacred: a single God, a traditional family, a strong work ethic, and a feeling of home that grew from the land. The epigraph of "To Lunar Shore" mentions the "thing of paradox," perhaps the human being, but perhaps something more akin to the "rough beast" of Yeats. The passage invites us to "decipher out the runes / upon these pages." Beyond the apparent contrast of technology and rural life, a further paradox may be poetry itself, which consumes the poet's energies in the flames of its making. McNeill imagines a manuscript tossed free of the destruction of the human race and beyond the home on the hilltop, as if memory, landscape, and creativity might help correct our potentially self-destructive course.

A major poem in this vein, here reprinted for the first time since the 1970s, is "Fireseed," McNeill's creation story. Informed by science and spoken in rhyming tercets of uncharacteristically dense language, she creates a mythic persona that speaks beyond time as it re-imagines the genesis of the earth and the life upon it. McNeill's formal skills, especially her use of repetition and parallelism, are well-suited to her vision. She begins with what appears to be cell division, but is rather like the organic world birthed from the inorganic, a distinctly non-Biblical genesis that moves in geometric progression to a vast diversity: "Thousands to millions; billions flame— / Out of the oneness, trillions came; / Out of the sameness, none the same." Caught in the sun's gravity, the earth's first orbit marks the beginning of geological time, followed by the formation of both plants ("xylem and cortex slowly grew") and minerals. In one of many paradoxes, coal becomes "ferned forever in its blackness, branched and veined / Trapping the sunlight, so contained / Fire forever with darkness skeined."

Following an unrhymed stanza imagining the formation of oil and then forsaking the tercets altogether, the poem launches a rhyming progression through animal and farm power to diesel, ending in cyclotrons and satellites, television screens and men on the moon. It seems to enact Einstein's famous equation by recognizing material forms as manifestations of raw energy. In the final stanza the rhymes disperse, the lines lengthen, and rhythms vary as the poem's pace, like civilization, accelerates. "God is the fire made manifold," the voice declares. A golden light from the far reaches of quasars is suddenly manifest in a "falling gratefire," evoking "primordial sunsets." McNeill's lines echo Whitman in their broad claims: "From one form to another I am passing," she announces, "I change but do not go." Naturally, she also speaks for the earth itself. Its diversity remains within the One, a belief stated with finality and without doctrinal vocabulary.

Since many of these poems were written after the atomic bombs ended World War II and simultaneously gave rise to the Cold War, they acknowledge the possibility of apocalypse, albeit one that appears nondenominational. If time moves in cycles, she seems to suggest, then even in our destruction and darkness, nature will provide. In "Potherbs," one survivor finds "the harsh nettle, the blade of the sedge, / The fern and the toadflax" and "hunt[s] for the pokeweed upon that burnt hill— / Burnt hill of the atom, hot dust of the cloud." The speaker remembers how knowledge of edible plants helped her ancestors survive. In "Life-Force," the speaker wanders the "rubble of earth" and invites Nature to impregnate her, to re-initiate the cycle of life on earth, which outlasts even apocalypse.

Other poems in this section reflect what commentators and physicists of the time, like David Bohm, Gary Zukav, and Fritjof Capra, were recognizing in the 1970s: that at the subatomic level and in the macro-cosmologies of astrophysics, the nature of reality may be revealed. The human aspiration to go beyond the circle of home and hearth, to explore within the grain of sand or upon the surface of the moon, leads only to a richer encounter with Creation. At every magnitude and distance, the new science suggests, the continuous miracle of consciousness is occurring, and McNeill's poems resonate with such awareness. "Chain Reaction" imagines the moment before the Big Bang, an "iron night" where a seed hangs and bursts. A soundless explosion becomes a metaphor for a flower in the poem's last, echoing word: "blooms." In another poem, she explores the nature of light in a language that meshes the scientific and the religious: "Resplendence and effulgence, radiance, gleam, / Splendor, illumination, and the stream, ineffable, of beauty / from the One." And her speaker goes on, perhaps because only God knows, to acknowledge the limits of our human conception and language:

Principles, models, properties, and forms:
Formulas, graphs, refractions, and the lens;
But never yet the Nature of defined;
The thing itself more primal than the things
In terms of which description might be tried.

And consider "Quadrille of the Naked Contours." At the end of material things, she imagines the "Absolutes" dancing with our abstractions, our "theorems," and with the scientific method itself. From the smallest quanta arise all things material and conceptual, which she calls the endless "skein of Paradox." In destruction is creation. And as a civilization moving forward at great speed, we may lose our sense of place, like the astronaut in "Lost in Orbit." The poem seems to lament that he has no earthly place to come to rest ("never a grave on the hilly ground") and hence no comfort.

The speakers of these poems have gone beyond the self and the landscape of home, seeking an understanding of nature or seeking other fulfillments, and that is the paradox of *Paradox Hill*: in our hollows we had everything we needed, but we wanted more. Louise McNeill's mature poetic vision recognizes that the far reaches seen from the top of that hill continue to intrigue. There is another life, from Charlotte to the Mare Imbrium and beyond, and some will leave these hills behind. But as she reminds us, we carry our pasts, like children, like landscapes, inside us, and they keep us whole along the way.

In preparing this slimmer edition of *Paradox Hill*, I selected poems that represent McNeill's considerable skills in verse as well as her rich understanding of the relation of the local to the universal. The original edition aimed to balance these tensions, to express an arc from the interior and familiar to the exterior and mysterious. While excising many poems that were repetitive of similar themes or which fell just short of McKinney's ideal fusion of beauty and toughness, I have tried to retain McNeill's deep understanding of the interaction of accelerating developments and the lasting Appalachian spirit. I have also preserved McNeill's original fastidious and occasionally idiosyncratic punctuation, including her Dickinson-like use of dashes to emphasize longer stops in the flow. Because it is a historical document as well as a collection of enchanting poems, this edition uses the original title for the poem "White Dwarf Stars," which McNeill's son, Douglas Pease, properly re-titled "Neutron Stars" for *Fermi Buffalo*. "The Martian Box" was also re-titled (as "A Scientific Experiment: The Construction of a Martian Box") in that volume.

The idea of re-collecting *Paradox Hill* and bringing this memorable book back into print came from Patrick Conner, former director of the West Virginia University Press, and I am indebted to him. Many thanks also to Carrie Mullen, the new director, and to Hilary Attfield and Rachel Rosolina for their patience and help in preparing this edition. My own understanding of McNeill's work owes everything to poets and scholars whose recognition of McNeill's genius precedes my own: Maggie Anderson's introduction to *Hill Daughter* as well as essays by Irene McKinney, Ken Sullivan, and Larry Groce, which appeared in a reprinted edition of *Gauley Mountain* (Pocahontas Communications Cooperative, 1996). William Plumley, late of the University of Charleston, and Devon McNamara of West Virginia Wesleyan College have long supported McNeill's work, and Arthur Buck's unpublished study "Louise McNeill's Expanding Vision" was also very helpful. Thanks to Marshall University colleagues Chris Green, whose own research on McNeill was invaluable, to Katharine Rodier and Shirley Lumpkin, for help and encouragement, and to John McKernan, editor of *ABZ*, which reprinted several of McNeill's poems. The Graduate College of Marshall University, specifically Dean Leonard Deutsch, provided generous faculty-development support toward the completion of this project. The West Virginia State Archives provided access to several reviews of the original edition of *Paradox Hill*. And thanks always to Ron Houchin, whose belief in the spirits of our antecedent voices carries the poetry forward.

Arthur E. Stringer
Huntington, West Virginia
December, 2008

Appalachia

STORIES AT EVENING

(A suburban mother tells stories to her son)

"My great great grandpa Jethro walked
The wild savannahs deep in grass;
He saw the herds of buffalo
File westward through the mountain pass.

"Great grandpa William in his time
Remembered pigeons wild and gray
Whose thousand wings beat out the sun
The morning that they flew away.

"My grandpa Frederick could recall
The wild trout flashing in their school;
He set his stick of dynamite
And scooped a hundred from the pool.

"My father, Douglas, saw the trees.
Across this bare, eroded land,
He saw the tulip tree and ash,
The spruce and hemlock—virgin stand.

"And I myself at morning saw
The chestnut on the ridge—its living green—
The blue-fringed gentian . . .

"Listen, now, my son—
Stories at evening—wonders I have seen;
And, as we sit, look sharp and well remember—
Your son may hear the strangest tale of all:
How little rabbits hopped across our garden,
How *grass* grew by the wall,
And there, one night, when you were six or seven,
You heard a Bob White call."

THE ROADS

(Appalachia)

Where do the roads go—
The ruined country roads flow,
Fern-clogged and weed-bogged, wandering the hills?
Nowhere that I know—by shad-blow and fence-row,
By woods where the lilacs grow,
By the rotted sills.

What can a road feel?
How can this sorrow heal?
Sole mark and wagon wheel passing through the day,
Grain load and apple load creaking down the hilly road—
All of the life that flowed—
Now gone away.

Where do the roads wind?
What do they go to find—
Crossing on the mountain tops and meeting by the shores,
Swamp-locked and briar-blocked, searching for the rib-rocked
Men of the mountain stock,
By their empty doors—

Frost pocked and burr-docked.
Winding through the passes
Where the dying chestnut trees reach their shriveled arms—
Thorn-crossed and time-lost, through the tangled grasses—
All the little country roads,
Searching for the farms. . . .

BALLAD OF PETE ELLERS

The name of Ellers was one to speak
Among the farmers of Red Hawk Creek.
Two thousand acres of cattle land,
And herds that carried Ellers' brand.

The widow Kramer, whose shanty stood
Next Ellers' line fence across the wood,
Had half an acre, three guinea fowl,
A flock of chickens, a dog to howl.

When old man Ellers took sick and died,
Young Pete, at twenty and in his pride,
Got all the holdings—an only son,
And meanness in him since time begun.

Just plain, born meanness it was in Pete,
As if the Devil—He like to beat
His bulls and horses, would take a chain
And stand there lashing, and lash again,
To cut the blood out; then laugh to hear
The wild horse-whicker, to smell the fear.
It gave him pleasure, so it would seem,
To watch things suffer and hear them scream.

By Widow Kramer's there was a spring—
Unfailing water, a precious thing
In cattle country. Young Pete was set
At first to purchase, but when he met
The Widow's silence, he went to court
And wangled somehow by deed and tort,

With land re-survey and lawyer tongue
To oust the Widow. When she still clung
To shack and springhouse and would not budge,
Young Pete went bragging how he would nudge
That squatter woman. She'd change her tune
About his cowspring—and Goddam soon.

One night that winter Pete filled his hide
With rotgut whiskey and took a ride
Across the woodlot, but soon returned . . .
At Widow Kramer's a shanty burned;
The hens all cackled, the guineas cried;
But Widow Kramer, until she died
Upon the County, could never speak—
Her mouth would open, her throat would creak,
But no sound from it; nor could she spell
Upon her fingers and terror tell.

But Ellers' fortune was fortune still.
He married money and had his will
And seven children—five feisty sons—
The name of Ellers—for so it runs:
On earth the Mighty and not the Meek;
If Justice rankles, it does not speak.
—And lived till eighty—The night he died
When midnight answered, the guineas cried—
Old Ellers screaming—and screamed to draw
The window curtains—outside he saw—
They pulled the curtains—but far too thin;
Old Widow Kramer kept looking in.

BALLAD OF THE REST HOME

I saw four silver ponies
Come swimming in from the sea,
And on the four, across the shore,
My loved ones came to me.

I leaned out from the window;
I called—they heard me call:
The nurses came and took me;
They stood me by the wall.

I saw the gray wall open;
I saw them all again;
I saw *five* silver ponies
Come rising from the main.

The fifth was newly bridled;
His feet were nailed with fire;
I took my match and lit it
And waited in the pyre.

My pony stood before me;
I mounted him and turned;
The others rode beside me,
And all the glory burned.

We rode the waves at sunset;
And so they took me home. . . .
At dark, five silver ponies
Went down into the foam.

BALLAD OF NEW RIVER

The prehistoric New River—called by geologists the "Teays"—once ran from North Carolina, north and west, into Illinois, where it received the tributary waters of the ancient Mississippi and then flowed south to a pre-historic embayment of the Gulf. When the glaciers melted, the western section of the river was dammed behind silt walls and "captured" by the Ohio. Today the eastern section of the New still flows in its primordial channel.

Ancient of rivers—called the New—
Oldest of all earth's streams—
Flowing here when *Tyrannous Rex*
Walked in his lizard times.

Glaciers melted, the silt walls washed,
Damming the westward run.
The river turned like a captured beast;
The Ohio gulped it down.

But west of the capture, the New was old,
River of earth and time,
Moving on through the shadowed wild,
Deep in its canyoned flume.

The bison came to the waterside,
And the wild swans floated still;
The Cherokee and the Shawnee brave
Passed by on the river trail.

The white men trekked by its rocky shores—
The lean, tall, hunter men—
The frail canoes on its current rode,
And the ox-bowed wagons ran.

The wagons crossed as they trundled west;
Then the soldiers, gray and blue,
Bled out their lives in the river's mist,
And the railroads tunneled through.

The boats of oil and the boats of coal
Slugged past on the river's weight;
The forests fell, and the logs swept down
When the elder bloom was white.

Sulfur water and tannery ooze,
And the black, raw sewage crawled;
The New moved on through its stinking maze,
Heavy and rank and coiled.

* * * * *

Lizards may go and lizards return,
And the hominids depart,
But the New flows on through the oak and fern
Of the forest's mended heart.

Ancient of rivers—called the New—
Oldest of all earth's streams—
Flowing now where *Tyrannous* stalks,
Raising his lizard combs.

BALLAD OF MISS SALLY

Miss Sally lay on her cornshuck bed,
Old and alone and poor,
In her tumbled shack on the Buck Thorn hill,
With dirt for its kitchen floor.

Miss Sally lay on her cornshuck bed.
She was dying of gangrene;
For she'd broke her hip, and she'd crawled to bed,
And the neighbors had not seen.

The neighbors came, and they found her there,
And they called Relief in town;
Relief-man came to Miss Sally's house
And his money blank laid down.

"Sign your papers?" Miss Sally laughed,
"I've silver to do and more;
A hundred thousand my father left,
And it's hid in the kitchen floor."

The neighbors came, and they called Relief,
And after the things they said—
The health nurse came with her laundry sheets
To put on Miss Sally's bed.

"Keep your sheets for I have my own—
And all of the linen fair:
Forty sheets in my mother's press,
And it's locked in the corner there."

The neighbors came with their gifts of food.
"Plenty I keep myself,
Bread and honey and golden cream,
All hid on my cupboard shelf."

The doctor came to Miss Sally's house,
For he knew Relief would pay.
"Cures I mix in my old black pot,
And I'll walk at the dawn of day."

SCOTCH IRISH

In Appalachia—our family graveyards—
Where all the headstones standing face the east—
Of Keltic blood, when Stonehenge was the portal,
Our fathers' fathers watched the Druid priest . . .

Bring me at morning to our weedy hilltop;
With all my pagan kindred lay me there—
The wine is crimson in the spiles of sunlight;
The priest intones the prayer . . .

Liter by liter down my life stream running—
The blood and fog and flame—
Remembering when Stonehenge was the portal
Before the Roman came.

MEMORIA

I have never heard them;
I shall never hear—
Still an echo falling
When the night is clear,
In the darkness wakes me
Like a trumpet's call:
Wild swans crying
Southward in the fall.

HILL DAUGHTER

Land of my fathers and blood, oh my fathers, whatever
Is left of your grudge in the rock, of your hate in the stone;
I have brought you at last what you sternly required that I
    bring you,
And have brought it alone.

I, who from the womb must be drawn, though the first born,
    a daughter,
And could never stand straight with the rifle, nor lean with
    the plow;
Here is ease for the curse, here is cause for the breaking of silence.
You can answer me now.

It has taken me long to return, and you died without knowing,
But down where the veins of the rock and the aspen tree run—
Land of my fathers and blood, oh my fathers, whatever
Is left of your hearts in the dust,
I have brought you a son.

FIRST FLIGHT

Once when I was little and played on the hill,
One wondrous evening, I dream of it still—
Mom called me to dinner, impatient, I knew—
So I lifted my arms up and flapped them and flew.

I lifted my arms and flapped them, and, lo!
I was flying as fast as my short legs could go.
The hill swirled beneath me, all foggy and green;
I lit by the yard fence, and no one had seen.

I told them at dinner, I said, "I can fly."
They laughed, not believing. I started to cry
And ran from the table, and sobbed, "It is true—
You need not believe me: I flapped and I flew."

I told them next morning; I told them again—
For years I kept telling: they laughed and I ran—
No one would believe me; I ceased then to tell;
But still I remember, remember it well—

One soft summer evening up there on the knoll,
Before life had harried the reach of my soul,
I stood there in twilight, in childlight, and dew—
And I lifted my arms and flapped them and flew!

LIMESTONE CAVERN

Under the earth as under the waves,
The sea things sleep in the limestone caves;
The seaweed left on the shore alone—
The shell and its music turned to stone.

SEA AND FIRE

Hill locked and land locked,
A gingham child in my bare feet,
I stood by the meadow
On a cloud-scud day,
The shadow running
Over the grasses' tide,
Where I dreamed an ocean.

* * * * *

Now, by the shore,
A nylon lady
On a dirty beach where the kelp washes,
I dream of a bluegrass field
Where the wind followed.

* * * * *

My father, a sailor lad
Come home to the furrow
Of earth and the land rock—
Spinning his sea tales there—
Old in the firelight weaving—
The back log's flame—
Fire of the ship's wake—
Gold phosphorescence—

I remember the wrath of the firedog's faces—

Remember the leaping sails
Of the orange flame-oak on
The hearth of Ulysses.

WALK IN AUTUMN

Red brown and frosted sear
The sage grass cries
Down windy tunnels by the broken weir,
Keening that summer dies.

Let us go home—our hands together clasp
So frost can never break nor time remove
This little magic, certain to the last,
Whose trusted name is Love.

Let us go home—the bitter meadows whine,
Keening and calling of eternal snow.
Between our hands we hold life's surest sign,
Love, let us go.

THE ROADS

(Rocket-trail)

Over these hills so a foot might travel
Indian trail and buffalo trace,
And mile after mile of the laurel to unravel,
And westward at evening the path of a race.

Over these mountains the dug road was broken
By ax and by oxen was widened and drawn
Up ridge and down river—the wheel was the token—
The bow-covered wagons creaked west in the dawn.

A new road is climbing far over the ranges:
A white road, a jet-road, a trail still aglow—
A highway from earth, from the earth as it changes—
Worldward at evening the young men go.

THE SAILOR

My father at the last was blind,
And yet forever he could find
Continents cradled in his mind—
Continents, islands, shores, and grails
Far in the distance. Now he sails
Outward forever through the gales—

I stood beside him the day he went;
The wind came running; the canvas tent
Over his grave on the hill was rent
From off its moorings; it billowed fast,
And so my father went forth at last
Over his oceans of the vast

    Continents, islands, shores, and seas—
    My father sails through Eternities.

GARDEN MOMENT

Forty years I lived,
Never saw before
What I saw this morning,
And if forty more—
Though I watch forever,
Straining patient eyes—
Shall I see such other
Miracle arise:
See the brown earth cracking—
Rupture of the night—
And the seed, the flower,
Rising to the light.

ARROW GRASSES BY GREENBRIER RIVER

Arrow grasses by the river,
Phalanx, spear by spear arrayed,
Teach us that we may remember
Others here have walked afraid.

Teach us—all our generation—
We are not the first to know
Death and war and red transgression
Where these quiet waters flow.

Long ago our father's father
Here in springtime dropped his corn,
Died and fell, an arrow winging
In his heart that April morn—

Dead as you and I will ever
Lie beneath the atom's burst—
Arrow grasses by the river,
Teach us we are not the first,

Nor the last to live in danger,
Live in wonder and in woe,
Here on earth beside the river,
Where the quiet waters flow.

INVOLVED

(*The Spider*)

Lying on the hilltop
In the grasses tall,
Forest of the grasses
And myself so small,
Underneath the grass trees
In the sunny shine,
I saw the biggest spider
With eyes as big as mine:
And they were growing larger still,
For in them I could see
A little, tiny brown girl
Who looked like me;
And in her little brown eyes
I saw a spider crawl,
And in that little spider's eyes
A girl so very small
I just could see her eyes glint,
And in the glint there shone
A little, wee spider
Staring all alone. . . .
He stared at me so softly
I jumped up to run
And stepped on a spider mite;
Then blood was in the sun—
A little spot of mite blood
On the grasses' shine,
And in that blood a little drop
Of blood as red as mine.

BLIZZARD

In the blizzard night,
Bringing the cattle down from the hills,
We heard in our capped ears
The soundless screaming,
Sniffed in the ripped air the scent that has no smell,
Felt with our gloved fingers
The stiff bone formless and white,
Saw with our whipped eyes the shape unshadowed—

Only our blood recalled,
And the cattle calling
Answered the fear up there on the primal hilltops,
Where the frost grass whined,
And the naked thing crouched waiting.

SNOW ANGELS

Martin, Stevie, and Joe, and I,
Four in our family, long ago,
One winter day on the road to school,
Boot-top high through a field of snow,
Stopped by the old black walnut tree;
And Joe and Martin and I, all three,
Lay on our backs in a laughing row,
Our white forms printed. The tall one Joe;
Mart beside him; the fat one, me.
Then we called to Stevie, "Look yonder, see,
Angels resting beneath the tree!"

But Steve had paused by the open spring,
Down on his knees in the yellow mud,
Watching his face in the troubled pool
Where the snow birds drank and the cattle trod—
"Look, Steve, angels." But he just stepped
His muddy tracks where the angels slept.

Mart and Stevie and Joe and I,
Four in our family, long ago.
Then three white winds past the walnut tree—
And Joe and Martin and I, all three—

For pollen scatters; the leaf must blow;
The winged seed follow the squall of snow—
The winged seed follow, the field lie clear—

　　　(Mart in China, a card last year—
　　　Joe in Houston, a yacht and plane—

And here by the mirror I left my hands,
Binding my throat with a velvet chain—
The skin of my throat and the sharpening bone.)

Wind past the tree and the snow-whirls blown—
In the hands of our angels the wheat seed sown;
Over their bodies the wheat stalks mown.

But Stevie's tracks from the meadow spring
Still break the stubble and print the clay,
And his steps zig-zag with the cradle's swing,
So near the place where our angels lay.

One earth-born shape with his shoulders low—
Four in our family, long ago.

THRENODY FOR OLD ORCHARDS

There is such sorrow here in these old orchards
That had I, of the Greek, some darker strain,
These *stadia* of hills should curve to answer,
And I would rant the echo of my pain.

Here was the fruited tree-land of my fathers,
And here the bended bough-land of the fall,
And here the winesap bending, and the pippin,
And here the heartwood growing—and the gall. . . .

Gone is that time, and gone my orchard country,
And all the fields and farmsteads of this plain;
And all so lost—so lost;—the hardhack tangles,
And nettles choke the footpath and the lane—

And all so lost—and all so lost forever—
That had I, of the Greek, some tragic song,
Here, from the sounding well of this old orchard,
I would inflict my wrong
On all the world, and all the world would answer,
And, draped in hairy garments, walk the stage
And cry the death of kinsmen and of orchards,
And rage and rage and rage.

FOX AND GEESE

Let us make a circle here—
Round and round we go
Till our feet have made this ring
Beaten in the snow.

Let us cross it now with paths—
Criss-cross passing by,
Back and forth, until our trails
Cut it like a pie.

Let us play at Fox-and-Geese,
Run and chase and sing,
Play the world is still at peace,
And our world a ring
Made by children in the snow of this meadow long ago,
Children of the sun and snow—
Children of the sun.

OVERHEARD ON A BUS
(Miner's Wife)

"He must go down in the mine—
It's all he knows;
Certain as morning shine
Then off he goes—
Me standing there in the door
A-seeing black
And wondering evermore
If he'll come back. . . .

Asked him, I have, to quit.
I can beg and whine,
But there's nothing to do for it,
It's the mine, the mine—
And him cast under its spell,
So off he goes—
Black as the mouth of hell,
And when it blows—
But I reckon they pay him well,
And it's all he knows. . . ."

OVERHEARD ON A BUS
(Woman with a cleft palate)

"My husband up and left—gone away.
But me, I'm keeping on. I work by day.
It's my old Dad-in-law. He's not my own,
But still I call him 'Pa'—
Eighty-five and down in bed—
Sort of touchy. It's his head.
But Pa—well, he—
Always say he treated me
Good enough. It's turn about—
It's hard, they tell me;
Say, to put him out.
But I ain't got no people of my own."

MAYAPPLE HILL

Children warned against the Mandrake—
Apple of the twisted root,
On the hilltop every summer,
Suckle at the golden fruit;
Suck the pale exotic fragrance,
Revel in the mellow pome—
Children, drunken with the sunlight,
In the evening stagger home—
Nor at bedtime sense the fever,
Nor at morning any chill—
Taken from the tumored apple,
Golden on the August hill.

* * * * *

All the children of the summer
Sleeping drowsy in the sun
Of the upland, August meadow—
With their golden fevers done—
Children of the earth who reveled
In the sweetness of the fruit—
Lying with their limbs disheveled
In the Mandrake's twisted root—
Children of the twisted torsos,
Lying always, oh, so still—
Where the Mandrake's tumored apples
Ripen mellow on the hill.

HEART-WOOD

"Oak on the hill blew down last night—
Heart-wood rotten—it had to go—
A thousand years—it was there at dusk,
But this morning, no.

"Went out to the barn to feed the stock—
Noticed the wind was chill,
But I never thought, then I looked up there—
And there was the—hill.

"Stopped and set my fork in the snow—
Opened the gate, fed Prince his hay,
Put my hand on his neck and said,
'Gone with the old men—gone away.'

"Went back to the house to warm.
Said to Mary, 'There's been a blow—
Old oak tree on the hill is down,
Heart-wood rotten—it had to go.'"

BLUE AND BROWN

My father's eyes were dark and clear:
Within their iris orbs the sphere
Of earth expanded when he gazed
Above his hill-encumbered ways
And saw beyond the pasture swales
The westward sinking of the sails—
Ulysses homing through the gales.

My mother's eyes were still and blue:
Within their iris sunlight grew,
Then faded softly, growing small
To glimpse the roses on the wall,
To mend the pillow's edge of lace,
Or dust the nutmeg and the mace
Upon the piecrust's rounded face.

GRAVITY

When I was coasting on the hill,
One winter morning long ago—
I went so fast the earth was still,
And all the clouds were whirling so
I left the earth and took the air
And might be, still be, rising there
Had not a woodpile and a tree
Come falling *up* and met with me.

PASTURE LINE FENCE

Worry at night how I can fence the pasture—
Three mile at least—all up side-hill and down—
And wire so high—I looked in Sears and Roebuck
And asked them at the hardware up in town.
When work and rails was cheap, our granddad fenced it;
But that was 80—nearly—years ago—
A good rail fence, but long since sagged and rotted—
I just don't know.

My father, though he tried, could never make it,
With all the price of fence and wire gone so high—
Our chestnut dead for posts, so he would stake it
And patch it up with thorn bush—getting by—
And now *my* turn. I patch—the cattle wander
Over on Charlie Hinkle's. He's the same
And got no fences—all our mountain pastures
All run together cross-wise. It's a shame.
But still I think at night, and think, still keeping
How I can put a fence up—good and high—
As though old men could make it better sleeping
Out there upon the gravehill where they lie.

THE OLD WOMAN

Something a farmer learns in his life
Is to live with the weather—just like an old wife—
Tired of her crochets but proud half the way
Of his cranky old woman who works every day.

If it's sunshine he's wanting, why rain she thinks best;
If it's south wind he calls for, she sends him the west;
But season by season, a faithful old spouse—
She works and she briggles—The Earth is her house.

OVER THE MOUNTAIN

When I was a child and we lived at home
In our farmhouse under the mountain's comb,
The meadows stretched from our wide front door,
And the fields ran down to the river's shore;
But behind our house, to the west and north,
The mountain reared, from the earth reared forth—
A king of dark, with a rocky crown,
The mountain stood, and its dark fell down
In shadowed length on our wide front door,
And across our fields to the south and shore.

When I was a child and we lived and grew,
My four tall brothers had work to do
And hills to run when their work was through;
But I, the dreamer, and of them all
The only sister so lone and small,
Was always different since I was born,
My one leg twisted like gnarly thorn—
Four tall brothers, but I the lorn
Child who sat by the back-yard tree
And staring, staring, could almost see
Across the mountain and over far,
North and westward by wind and star.

"Over Bonnie"—the tales they told—
When I was little, the words were gold:
"Bonnie River" and "Over Yon,"
"Across the Mountain" and on and on
Where I had never, *have* never gone.

My four tall brothers and Gramp and Pa
Ran the ridges and rooked the law,
And every June time and every fall,
At brook trout rising and turkey call,
Crossed the mountain, I watched them fade
Up morning ridges, through tear-mist shade
Until they vanished; yet leaf-tread still
I walked behind them down Galford hill,
Across the hacking, through rocky gate;
The pine wind touched me—my leg was straight.

A week. I waited. One sunset burned;
The six tall hunters that night returned,
Dropping downward through files of gloom,
With trout and turkey and wild bee comb—
"Mama, Mama! It's them, come home!"

* * * * *

When I was a child—as I am no more,
For I left my place by our backyard door,
And east and south were the fields stretched wide,
South and east by the river's side,
Where long, green meadows, swinging glide—
I found my city, my brace, my pride.
Found this city . . . so bright and bare,
But still at evening on street and stair,
When stars moved over, I always yearned
North and westward. When starlight burned
Above the smokestacks, I turned my eyes—
King and Monster, I saw it rise

Above my city, my safe-lit town—
That hill of granite, that rocky crown.

* * * * *

On penthouse roof and at the subway gate,
I turned, and turn, and always, soon or late,
As now, this evening still . . . for visions do fulfill,
Arising not at will, but of themselves, by power yet unknown . . .
And I have walked, a thousand nights, that hill,
Beneath my feet each loved, familiar stone,
And known, by heart, the pathways where they wind,
So well that I could walk them with the blind,
And find, and surely find. . . .
      I know that country . . . every brake of laurel, the long
Savannahs, scent of pennyroyal, the pine wind blowing—
Waters gray and wild
And always farther, farther—dream-beguiled—
Across to Bonnie River—undefiled.

* * * * *

In some strange room when ether brings the night
In waves descending downward on my sight,
Then I will track my hunters—gone before—
And all lean, lawless hunters of that shore—
Beyond the mountain, through the rocky crown,
Across the green savannahs flowing down
In tides of bluegrass westward where they roll—
Forever, farther, farther—"Bonnie Shoal."

Scattered Leaves

REFLECTION WITHOUT COLOR

Black God on the black cross, white Christ upon the tree,
Sloe-eyed God whose hands are yellow,
Red Sun whom the red men follow,
Brown-skinned Jesus by the sea,
Who, in heaven, fashioned me?

All my kind—in every land: members of a doubtful race,
Who have never seen God's image
Crowned with stars or feathered plumage;
Never seen His form or face
Rising from the winds of space—

In His image we were made. In His likeness formed divine.
I am white, but you are yellow;
You are gold, but I am sallow;
Search the pale prismatic line—
Is God's color yours or mine?

Then what substance are we of? Like to God's and His unknown?
Crystal blood? Transparent fiber?
See the moonlight like a sabre
Striking through our lucent bone—
Striking through us, brush the stone.

We are nothing; we are all—all whose pigments blend and fade.
Where we walk no fern is bended;
Through night's claws we slip unwounded,
Shadows passing into shade;
In God's image we are made—

Having neither shape nor color,
Immaterial as light,
And our only proof of living:
Breath upon the mirror moving—
On the mirror of the night.

TO THE BOYS IN FRESHMAN HISTORY
(Thermopylae—480 B.C.)

What can I tell you of the past
To guard you from the atom blast
Unless the story of that day
The Spartans stood to bar the way?

Two hundred thousand Persians flowed,
A pluméd river, up the road.
Three hundred Spartans, shield to shield,
To guard the passage—not to yield—
And yielded only one-by-one.
Old Sparta's children, son by son,
Struck upward, and the Persian fell;
For dearly bought what Spartans sell;
The harsh old Mother teaches well.

And now, forever, Greece is free,
And on the plains of Thessaly
The sheep crop softly in the grass,
The road winds upward through the pass,
The dust of Persia silts the sea,
The shepherd guards Thermopylae.

The Turk and Nazi both are gone,
From Thrace the eagle of the dawn
Wheels southward—and the silver gulls
Of Skyros bank above the hulls
Of Xerxes' drownéd Argosy,
A salted trestle in the sea—
And still, forever, Greece is free.

And so what better can I say,
But tell you softly of that day
The Spartans stood to bar the way?
For them the arrow's flaming hiss;
For you the atom's gentle kiss:
But I must tell you—*tell* you this.

THE DREAM

I tried to move,
  But I could make no motion;
I tried to scream,
  But all my screams were gone;
I tried to see,
  But fog was lapped around me—
I lay upon my face, yet saw my spine,
And every bone there seemed to shine—
My country's bones?
  Or were they mine?

Each vertebra a coin of gold
Set deeply in my flesh and skin —
Set deeply there and hammered in
Until because of gold—its love—
I could not move—
  I tried to move—

POET

I am trajectory and flight—
The archer, arrow, and the bow—
The swift parabola of light—
And I the rising and the flow,
The falling feather of the cock,
The point, propulsion, and the flood
Of blackbirds twanging from the nock,
And I the target and the blood.

THE CAVE

In the caverns, where light
Never filters through the night,
There the strange, albino things
Breed forever: bats with wings,
Leaf-veined fibers, thin as pearl,
And the blind worm's silver curl.

In the cave's unmottled dark,
There the white eel loops his arc,
There the blinded spiders spin,
Weaving, eyeless, out and in,
Catching frail, lactescent strands
In their whited spider hands.

Where the rivers of the mind
Subterranean must wind,
There the cobra rimed with snow,
Hooded, in the dark must flow;
And the wan iguana crawls,
Plated lily, down the walls.

THE GOLDEN GARDEN OF CUZCO

In the garden of the Inca,
In the Sungod's dying rays,
Made of beaten gold and planted,
Stood the shining stalks of maize—

Stood the shepherds with their llamas,
Golden boys and golden brutes;
Stood the field of golden grasses,
Golden vineyards, argent fruits;
Stood the vinetree of the roses,
Growing rootless, made of gold,
In the garden of the Inca—
But the light was turning cold,
And the soldiers of Pizzaro,
Just before that day was done—
Stopped to rest—and raped the virgins
In the temple of the sun.

EDEN TREE

Black fatal tree, whereof we tasted death;
Dark golden apple of our farthest care;
Harsh mate, fast growing by the tree of life,
Whom God made flourish there;—

For all the knowledge, both of good and ill,
Mankind has taken from your limber bough,
And for the stem where my own sorrow hung,
I give these praises now:

Leaf of your greenness open to the sun,
Trunk of your strength uplifted to the light,
I praise for beauty, but as surely praise
Your roothold in the night.

Bloom fair and fairer yet in Eden's walls,
Unpruned, untended, blossom there alone;
Though cursed by ages, still bring forth your fruit
Of knowledge and unknown;

And live immortal in a mortal's praise;
In every careful orchard, seed and grow;
And of sweet earth and water take your fill
For bearing of our woe.

WARNING

Walk through the fern but do not tear the root.
Rest on the stump but count no ring of age.
In rotting wood see neither hint nor sign,
Nor translate from the oak leaf's fallen page
One mystic line.

Look at the wheat field, see it blade and straw,
But neither bread nor sealed-in germ nor shadowy reaper—
Leave the close ground its anonymity,
Such knowledge to the blind mole and the worm—
The gray night-creeper.

Leave the enigma to the close-lipped dark;
Beyond your fenced-in land do not inquire—
For things there best be hidden:
Light that only the blind should see—
And over the hills in that far country
Truth bare, forbidden.

TIME—THE PASSAGE OF TIME

Kill the black cobra
Whose hood is the terror
Of loneness and darkness
And death in the mirror;

Kill the gold python
Who hangs in the forest—
Whose way is by winding
By nearest and dearest;

But fear the clear serpent
Transparent as morning
Who glides without color—
So soft is his turning

He flows on the grass,
And the grass is not flowing—
He breathes on the leaf,
And the leaf is not blowing.

CONFESSION

Oh, we your people are so small
We dig the burrow, build the wall
To shield us from the sparrow's fall,
And, in our prison, so distrust
The clean suggestion of the dust,
We guard the hangman, hang the just.

We tie our faith to little things:
Old cups and teapots, worlds and kings.
We anchor ships with linen strings,
And, faint of hope, dare not forsake
The four-lane boulevard to take
The wild road through the marshy brake.

BOATING SONG

Drift, drift, do not lift
Your birch pole from the river.
Let the arrow grasses grow
In their reedy quiver.
Let the arrow grasses grow
In their moveless shallow
Underneath the moon-strung bow
Of a leaning willow.

Drift, drift, do not turn
Near that clump of arrows.
On each side the fox-fires burn
Warning of the narrows.
Drift, drift, do not pause
Where those arrows sway.
Who would see them bring to earth
The dead, white bird of day?

THE INVISIBLE LINE

Mothers must draw a subtle line
Finer than any thread is fine;
Must firmly hold but never clutch,
Must freely give but not too much,
Must stand apart but never far,
Must heal the wound but bless the scar;
And falsely speaking, truly tell,
And, guarding, never guard too well;
And hearing, fail to overhear;
And fearing all things, have no fear;
And loving, love each child the best,
But no child dearer than the rest.

AUBADE TO FEAR

Last night as I lay cold with fear
Of my travail now drawing near,
A gray wind I no longer hear
Blew from the darkness over me—
Blew southward from the Norn-white skies
Until I slept with seeing eyes—
Seeing no bauble fit to prize.

Not seeing dawn, its thin gray trace
Turn gold upon the pillow lace
And touch the warm beloved face.
Not seeing all I lived to own:
The torque of rubies, stone by stone,
The living pages touched and known.

Seeing instead that nets are small
Which shield us from the sparrow's fall,
How frail the rooftree and the wall,
How thin the string by which we tie
Our great ships of the wind and sky—
And what a little thing to die.

MINUTIAE

Hill Song

      The ferns are in the fiddlehead, fiddlehead;
      The ferns are in the fiddlehead.
      The service tree in the woods is white;
      The wild crab sheds its fragrant light;
      The bullfrogs boom from the crick at night—
      And the ferns are in the fiddlehead.

Moment Caught at Twilight by a West Virginia Barn

      A rainbow curves between day and dark,
      And the swallows fly through the rainbow's arc.

Moment

      The firedogs guard my hearth tonight;
      A fallen forest embers there;
      Photons of enigmatic light
      Dispute my table and my chair.

Quatrain

      When the firedrake comes again,
      When the firefang eats the grain,
      Then extinguish my desire—
      Inundating fire with fire.

Vietnam

      Born in war and bred in war,
      My son, I hope you are ready for ———

Journey

      From her torture going free—
      Safe into insanity.

Couplet

> I write now of justice from where I am lain—
> This bone is my pencil, my tablet the rain.

Well Meaning

> Well meant! Well meant! Say that she meant so well
> She always brought good tidings out of Hell.

The Torque

> I dreamed the world was like a torque
> Of twisted space and twisted time—
> As I am of this torquéd race
> So bitter twisted—and sublime.

Must Be

> In the infinite worlds of expanding space,
> Where the suns swing out, and the quasar rolls—
> In the undimensions of time and place,
> There must be a star for souls.

Cold Comfort for the Population Explosion

> Lemmings leap into the sea—
> Caterpillars on the tree strangle softly—
> So will we.

My Enemy

> Who hated me, who did me wrong
> Until I wished him dead,
> And who, today, discomfits me
> By being as I said.

Axiom

    X

    Is sex.

Universal

    There is no Hell, but here on earth we pause,
    To spend vacations with our out-in-laws.

Riposte

    The depth of your smooth texture I divine,
    But not how your good conscience makes you mine.

Couple

    You have not changed—for Time is kind;
    Your face—to me—is never lined;
    As you grow wrinkled, I grow blind.

UNDER SEA—THE UNICORN

("Canst thou bind the unicorn with his band to the furrow?")

High on the mountains, under waves,
Where sea grass covers the sailors' graves,
Stands a forest; the sea ferns frond
The glade, and farther, the shade beyond,
Where blue sea holly and green sea fir
Tower over; the sea winds stir
Sea moss lichens, and mirrored leaves
Tremble softly; the sea dove grieves—

         *   *   *   *   *

Fields of the water wander low;
Over the meadows sea fans blow
And sea bats circle; their circles flow
Over the sea fans, under the gulls
Over the trestles of sunken hulls,
Bat wings circle.
            The unicorn
Rears in shadow, his silver horn
Gores the silence; he paws the hill
Under ocean; unharnessed still—
For he plows no furrow, he turns no sod—
Myth or substance, the Barb of God
Wears no halter; his hoof beats sound
Along the canyons that time has wound
Under ocean; he flashes, leaps
Over the sea firs, and down the steeps
Of sunken ranges; his flowing mane
Flays the rudder, dissects the chain,
Cleaves the tempest, divests the wind

Of all its rancor; the storm is thinned
Before his coming, the mystic one—
By waves distorted, he seems to run
Through broken rivers, by crackled moons,
Through old pulsations and lost monsoons,
Up vibrant meadows, through fractured sands,
Across mutations in shattered lands,
Down ruptured passes, through falling rings
Of undulations. All broken things
Of land and water deform his flight.
He is wholly darkness and surely light . . .
The thorn of sunrise
And the tusk of night.
He rears to northward; to southward turns—
The green Sargasso behind him burns,
And all seas seven, the Quantum Firth:
The Pole Star spinning revolves the earth
Around his antler—his flaming horn—
His tusk of darkness, and still unshorn;
For he plows no furrow, he turns no sod.
Over the mountains he runs for God—
Over the mountains his path is wild—
On his back
        He is bearing
            A human child.

To Lunar Shore

If somewhere in the cooling rocks
Of cosmic seas, of cosmic dunes,
You find this thing of paradox
And can decipher out the runes
Upon these pages edged with scorch,
Forgive their tinges of the fire;
I flung them like a riven torch
Above the rupture of the pyre;
They billowed in a greenish blast;
And, with them, belling far away,
I heard the hound dogs of the past
Upon the burning mountains bay.

OF SOOTHSAYERS

Above the Hanging Gardens, above the Euphrates,
Astarte rose, up-living, the goddess of Chaldees.
The wise men read the omens; the omens all were fair.
The gardens hung, the roses, eternal in the air.

The I.B.M. is spewing statistics from its mouth;
Orion rises northward: Astarte from the south.
The statistician ponders the omens of the card;
The Ziggurat has fallen, the holy vase a shard.

The statistician, reading, extrapolates with care;
The cherry blooms hang softly   blue Potomac air.

FIRESEED

Primordial space, Primordial dark—
One atom spinning in its arc,
The worldseed lonely as a spark—

Spinning and growing till it grew
Great in the silence; then it blew;
Out of the oneness, there were two—

Two in the vastness burned and whirled;
Four in the void forth were hurled:
Eight in the thunder—so a world—

Thousands to millions; billions flame—
Out of the oneness, trillions came;
Out of the sameness, none the same.

Trillions to trillions split and glowed;
All in accordance, out they rode;
Circle in circle burned and flowed . . .

Earth in its orbit cooled and spun
One first circle with time begun,
So forever to ring the Sun.

Fire winds passing spilt down a cell;
Ancient of oceans rose and fell
Washing branches of coral shell.

There in the swamplands fern seed blew—
Xylem and cortex slowly grew,
Giant rushes and strange bamboo.

Eons passing—the great trees died,
Fell and rotted; the serpents plied
Over that jungle undefied.

Ancient of oceans ebbed, returned—
Into the jungle sunlight burned,
Black, in its measures, coal was turned.

Ferned in its blackness, branched and veined
Trapping the sunlight, so contained
Fire forever with darkness skeined.

Gold, gold, and golden—
Golden monstrous snakes
Turning to oil, and winding through the earth,
Amber and iridescent through the caves,
Black, green, and tawny serpentines of oil
Enfolding waves of sunlight in their coil—
Gold, gold, and golden—
Trapped to flame again,
Wild on the steeps of derricks in the sky.

Another time—the years and days
In circles moving, and the rays
Of great wheels moving down the ways
Of sunlight; oxen in their yokes,
The great hubs turning and the spokes—
The oxen like a fire that stokes
The shining grasses of the plains;
The horse a fire that burns the grains

Of golden oat seed as he strains
To pull the plow. The Diesel turns
The oil of serpents as it churns,
So cycle into cycle burns—

Gold, gold, and golden—golden cyclotrons
Throb in the leadshields, while around the Earth
The kilowatts and ergs and quanta move
Intricate webs of fiber from the sun
Pulsing the engines. From the wilds of space
The satellite relays the colored forms
That burn and posture on our TV screens;
And down the dusty craters of the moon
Men stumble drunken, picking up the rocks.

Singing and seething from the core of wonder,
Consuming, unconsumed,
I pass undying through these globes of tinder
Candescent and illumed.

Gold, gold, gold, and gold—
Nothing is ever still and cold;
God is the fire made manifold—

Flames in the wind and flowers in the quasar—
The quasars outward roar
Expanding worlds, and from my falling gratefire
Primordial sunsets pour—

From one form to another I am passing—

I change but do not go—
Foxfire and firefly and pitchblende seethe within me—
Volcanoes through me flow—
The snakes of golden oil burn in my body,
My flesh is veined and branching with the fire,
From form to form I pass, forever burning
Along this arc, and filamented wire
Magnetic holds me to the sun's turning.
From path to path I, too, can pull the sun—
The seedfire is of life, and we are burning, burning
Within the burning ONE.

AFTER THE BLAST

Then night will come, though not the "sable" night,
Though not the dark, the "wished for balm," the still. . . .
But deathly brightness, thermo-neutron night,
Until some star-mad watcher on a hill,
Across the galaxies will peer and cry
That where there once was nothing in the sky,
Now there is flame beyond the southward horn—
A small, new planet, risen fully born
In one wild surge of green and glowing birth,
And looking at it, he will name it

Earth.

LIFE-FORCE

(With acknowledgment to John Donne)

Alone on the rubble of earth—all alone—
Alive in my body, and blood on the stone—
The black amanita, the hydrogen pall
Above me—I waken, and now I will crawl
For the woundwort to heal me,
For leaf and for shoot
To feed me; with water
I suck from the root
Of arum; with shelter
I claw from the dust;
And with life from the welter
To draw as I must;
I will wrap me in bindweed
And comb out my hair
With thorn from the thorn bush,
And southward repair
Across the burnt meadows,
And take to the wild—
Oh, sheath of the man-root
Beget me with child.

POTHERBS

(Of the edible wild plants my granny taught me.)

With fire to the eastward and fire to the west,
Then I may go hunting, with hunger possessed,
To break the harsh nettle, the blade of the sedge,
The fern and the toadflax, the flag on the edge
Of gullies, the crowfoot, the wild heron's bill;
I will hunt for the pokeweed upon that burnt hill—
Burnt hill of the atom, hot dust of the cloud—
If goose-grass is living, I will not be proud.

THE NEW CORBIES

If trees remain and carrion crows
Still gather on the oak,
That morning when the green wind blows
And carries off the smoke,
The crows will find below them there,
All blooming from the ground,
As flowered and as fat a feast
As crows have ever found.

Of scarlet red and bloated white,
And flowered full in bloom
Those tropic blossoms all will burst
To waft their sweet perfume.

And floating from the oak tree's limb,
Like hunger, then the crows
Will taste of man and savor him—
The richest fruit that grows,
When from the forehead of his dream
Exudes the atom rose.

PROPHECY FOR THE ATOMIC AGE

It is not *man* will tamp the fuse,
It is not *he* will plug the wire
To set this earth's dim little blast
Into the ruptured winds of fire.

It is not he—whose wondrous brain
Rots in the talons of the rose,
Whose pride becomes the lily's face—
Will send earth crumbling when she goes.

It is not he—who fails to read
In his own palm the holy trace;
It is not he—who fears to clasp
His brother in the market place—
Can send the smallest thing divine
Hurtling careless into space.

Bodies and caves he well may blast,
And rock the temple and the sea,
Eyes from their sockets still burst forth,
And leave blood drying on the tree—
These *he* may do—but to this speck of earth
Fasten yourselves prepared to journey far,
Knowing that only One shall rip her forth—
The Same who nailed the atom to the star.

AFTER HEARING A LECTURE ON MODERN PHYSICS

Where the atoms sing where the neutrons flow
In the mystic fog and the cosmic snow
A bell once rang where the cyclotron
In the midnight moves and the world moves on

A star once stopped on a desert bay
Where a stable stood where a child first lay
In the aureole of the vapored fire
And the shepherds heard from the bending choir
The atoms' song in the desert night
A red chief stood with his gourd of light
Where the mesa rose to the rising sun
Where the atoms sing
               and the worlds are one
And the worlds all sing on the singing wires
Of a million moons in the swinging fires
Of magnetic fields still the daisies move
In their meadow fields in the bending grove
Still the willows blow as in other years
The willows danced to the singing spheres
Now the forests sway to the atoms' chord
Where the rust is laid on a holy sword

The atoms move
             in the rusted blade
And the nightingales from a far-off glade
Sing out again where the cyclotron
In the midnight moves to the curving dawn

Where the music falls
          on magnetic strands
Angelic lutes in illumined hands
Once struck the note where the neutrons run
And the center glows and the worlds are one.

THE MARTIAN BOX
(After reading a Space experiment)

To hoax the stars, a box like Mars
    As hot and cold—and all controlled
        By thermostat and pressure gauge—
And then put microbes in the cage,
    And count by exponential rate
      The speed they grow at.

                    Thousands wait
      And die in Mars-cold.

                 Only three
       Survive the Martian degree;
And one of these, whose pedigree
    Is questionable

                (You will agree)
      Begins to flourish, more at home
      Than ever microbe in the loam
        Of earth-field prospered—

               So he grows
And reproduces—quickly goes through generations
    So robust and with such talent to adjust
      I view him with a cool distrust . . .

Invasion? Just suppose our fears
    Are running slightly in arrears
        (Perhaps by several billion years)
         And their arrival, cold or hot,
            Pre-dating Eden and the Grot,—
                Event propitious—when from Mars
                Our Pilgrims landed—
                    Oh my Stars.

THE LOVERS—SPACE AGE

There is no space—where do we walk
Along this stranded shore?
When time is nothing, need we talk
Of loving evermore?
The tide goes out but does not move,
And changeless shift the sands;
There is no moment here for love,
No touching of our hands.
In all immensity we wait,
And lost and burning cold,
Who, timeless, cannot now be young
And never will be old.

EARTH DAY—1970

The streams are running orange-red
With acid from the mines;
Car graveyards drip their metal guts
Half-tangled in the vines.

The air is thick with gob and dust;
Raw sewage chokes the sedge;
The contraceptive rubbers lie
Along the river's edge.

The strip mine is a stinking hole;
The oil slick clogs the sea;
This is the land our fathers loved
And "died to make it free."

WHITE DWARF STARS

Burned and white to the neutron bone
Dwarf stars stand in the night alone—
Dead white dwarfs with their fire-storms still—
I am burning and growing chill.

SPACE SHIP

When to the moon at the speed of light
I travel backward years in flight,
Arriving on that cratered dearth
Younger than when I left the earth—

When on to Mars I upward pass
By speed grown infinite in mass
In thickness nothing—like a droll
Shadow of self or else a soul—

When, to the star of farthest west
My journey over and to rest,
My space ship circles to that shore
Where round the endless waters roar

Then will I see that promised town?
Or touch the crater? Or the Crown?

PROJECTION TO A SPACE OF LOWER ORDER

Along the fourth dimension,
Where Time and Space have come
Co-ordinate together
In pure continuum,
> There is but one projection
> To indicate the sum:
> Extrapolate the silence
> And hang the darkness plumb.

LOST IN ORBIT

Lost in orbit and passed Earth by—
And on forever—around and round—
Over the tracks that the comets fly—
Searched forever but never found—
And never grow older and never die,
And never a grave on the hilly ground.

CHAIN REACTION

Primordial space—before there first was light—
And in the dark one utter density
Lost as a seed but concentrated down
To heaviness and potency, its weight
Hung in the iron night; and outward burst—
And burst again—and farther bursting still.

A chain reaction flaming forth the worlds
That spin and flash and thunder and expand
Forever outward in exploding blooms.

"LIGHT"

Photon or wave, bullet or billow riding?
One second seven-split around the earth;
Dual dilemma, paradox abiding, hiding the heart
Of flame-heart in the flame—

Here at this burning crux the mystics stood,
While on them through the ages, showers fell,
Full golden showers streaming always down and never upward:
Nimbus, halo, sun, the aura, aureole, glory, glance, and fire,
Resplendence and effulgence, radiance, gleam,
Splendor, illumination, and the stream, ineffable, of beauty
From the One, Godhead or Brahma, Sun God, or the Son
Of man uplifted—

Principles, models, properties, and forms;
Formulas, graphs, refractions, and the lens;
But never yet the *Nature of* defined;
The thing itself more primal than the things
In terms of which description might be tried.

QUADRILLE OF THE NAKED CONTOURS

At the end of night, and at end of day,
When the substance burns till it burns away,
And nothing stands by our burned-out seas
But some birches stripped to the soul of trees;
And nothing hangs in the upper zones
Of the crystal clear but the neutron bones
Of the white dwarf stars, like a ring of stones—
Then the Absolutes in their lucent cords
Will rise and dance on the burned-out swards.

Then the Theorems come, with their lines made clear
And the Formulae from the dark appear—
Then the Postulates and Hypotheses—
And the Zero drift from behind the trees
With its minus sign—and the Circle roll
And close itself, in itself made whole. . . .

Then the constant "h" with its frigid thews—
And the Quanta flow with their retinues—
Transparent forms—in that utter still
Will move and dance in their cold quadrille—
Abstractions' host—and the neutron bones
Of the white dwarf stars, like a ring of stones—

And then, and then, from the neutron rocks
Will rise the skein of the Paradox.

EARTH DAY 1971

Evoke the Earth—bring forth its flowing rivers:
The Congo and the Volga and the Stone,
Ohio, New, Kanawha, Mississippi,
The Drina and the Neva and the Rhone;
The Amazon, the Rio, the Missouri,
The Niemen and the Po,
The Deerfield, Susquehanna, Juniata,
McKenzie and Hwang Ho.

Evoke the Earth—lift up its serried mountains:
The Himalayas and the Apennines,
The Pyrenees, the Andes, and the Rockies,
The Zagros and the Pines;
The Altai and the Alps, the High Sierras,
The Caucasus, the Gauley, Great Cascade,
The Ozarks and the Lost, the Appalachians,
Lift up their rocks and shade.

Evoke the Earth—send out its seas and oceans:
Pacific and Atlantic, North and Red,
Aegean, Adriatic, South, and Baltic,
The Kara and Sargasso and the Dead.

Evoke the winds—the winds that blow upon it;
The Northwind and the Southwind, East and West,
Monsoon, Chinook, the Trade winds and Sirocco,
And all the winds that blowing never rest.

* * * * *

The bluegrass running purple down the meadows,
The brakes of laurel and cane,
The Steppes, the Veld, the Moor, the desert burning,
The cataracts of sunlight and of rain—

This living planet set in gentle motion,
This country of our birth,
This Island in Space-Time's unconstant ocean,
Evoke—the *Earth*.

LETTER WRITTEN AT TWILIGHT

Tired men of every nation,
Wherever you may be—
On burning plain or hill top
Or on the burning sea—
One moment pause at twilight there
And stretch your hands with me.

For now the rain has come at last—
The cool and silver calm,
Whose simple meaning of the past
Is now our only balm;

So where you are in all the earth,
Whoever you may be—
One moment pause at twilight there
And stretch your hands with me,

And stretch them forth as brothers do—
As brothers now in pain—
As brothers stretch our hands to bless
The falling of the rain. . . .

About the Authors

LOUISE MCNEILL was born in 1911 in Pocahontas County, West Virginia, on a farm that has remained in her family for nine generations.

McNeill received her early education in rural schools to which she later returned as a teacher. She graduated from Concord College and then received her master's from Miami University in Ohio. She earned a doctorate from West Virginia University and studied at Middlebury College with the poet Robert Frost, and at the Iowa Writers' Workshop.

Louise McNeill began her publishing career selling short poems to the *Saturday Evening Post* and went on to publish in such magazines as *Atlantic Monthly, Harper's,* and the *Christian Science Monitor.* Her first collection, *Mountain White,* appeared in 1931, and she went on to publish six other collections.

In the 1939 introduction to *Gauley Mountain,* Stephen Vincent Benet wrote "Miss McNeill has taken a part of the Amer-ican scene that most of us know little about and made both its past and its present come alive. . . . She sings as naturally as her people speak and there is both salt and melody in the tune."

McNeill taught English and history for over 30 years, retiring in 1973 to devote time to her writing. She and her husband, Roger Pease, named their son Douglas after her father, renowned Pocahontas County educator G. D. McNeill.

Louise McNeill was West Virginia's poet laureate from 1979 until her death in 1993. Upon her appointment, then-Governor Jay Rockefeller noted "she has captured the cadence of the language and the history of our people in volumes of poetry which poignantly bespeak our heritage."

A. E. STRINGER is the author of a collection of poems, *Channel Markers* (Wesleyan University Press). His work has appeared in such journals as *The Nation, Antaeus, The Ohio Review, Denver Quarterly, Shenandoah, Poetry Northwest, The Cincinnati Review, Kestrel,* and *ABZ,* and in two recent anthologies, *Wild Sweet Notes* and *Backcountry: Contemporary Writing in West Virginia.*

He has presented readings in a wide range of American locales and also in Galway, Ireland. A new collection of his poems, *Human Costume,* is forthcoming from Salmon Poetry of Ireland.

For twenty years, he has taught writing and literature at Marshall University where he directs the Visiting Writers Series.